RIDDLES & RHYMES

For Kids, Parents & Educators

CHRISTIAN THEMES

By Anita Vermeer, M.Ed.

Dedication:

This book is dedicated to all the passionate people that devote so much of themselves to supporting young children. A special thank you to those educators who work directly with the children. Your love and dedication to supporting the range of individual needs is remarkable.

Copyright © 2022 Anita Vermeer

ISBN: 978-1-7361353-4-1

All rights reserved. No part of this book may be reproduced in any form without permission from the author or publisher, except as permitted by U.S. copyright law. To request permission contact AnitaVermeer27@gmail.com.

Page intentionally left blank.

RIDDLES & RHYMES

For Kids, Parents & Educators

CHRISTIAN THEMES

By Anita Vermeer, M.Ed.

Table of Contents

Why this book 5

    Potential Learning Objectives: 6

    Instructional Ideas: 6

    Additional Ideas for Parents (or Educators): 8

Riddle Themes: 9

    Adam and Eve's Garden 10

    Christmas 12

    Daniel and the Lion 14

    David and Goliath 16

    Easter 18

    Jonah and the Whale 20

    Moses 22

    Noah's Arc 24

    Fall 26

    Winter 28

    Spring 30

    Summer 32

    Weather 34

Which Rhymes Matching Activities 36
- ADAM AND EVE'S GARDEN 37
- CHRISTMAS 38
- DANIEL AND THE LION 39
- DAVID AND GOLIATH 40
- EASTER 41
- JONAH AND THE WHALE 42
- MOSES 43
- NOAH'S ARC 44
- FALL 45
- WINTER 46
- SPRING 47
- SUMMER 48
- WEATHER 49

Word Card Matching Game 51
Answers 79
About the Author 81

Why this book

Young children are naturally curious, and these rhyming riddles provide an engaging way to embed imagination and captivate their attention. Children become more interested when they know there is a missing word at the end of each riddle to solve.

As an educator or a parent, you know that for most children, their learning will be reinforced when curiosity is connected to learning objectives. To support this, adults can be explicit about learning objectives when using this book with children. For example, just reading these riddles with children may or may not teach them that words rhyme, but explicitly labeling the words that rhyme may support that learning.

Children may also develop metacognition skills through these explicit forms of modeling. Therefore, regardless of how you decide to use this book, I encourage you use language such as: "Oh, I noticed, those words rhyme, house and mouse."

Potential Learning Objectives:

- Children will recognize and identify words that rhyme

- Children will use a word to rhyme with another word given to them

- Children will use deductive reasoning skills to solve the riddles

- Children will use rhyming skills to solve the riddle

- Children will build conceptual knowledge on similar topics

- Children will build new vocabulary and descriptive language

Instructional Ideas:

Many of the ideas below are tailored for the classroom. However, parents can easily make some minor adjustments to using them at home. For example, a morning message can be posted on a kitchen refrigerator just as easily as it is can be posted on a chart paper in a classroom. Some ideas can be embedded into large or small group activities, or some may work better through individual settings. The needs of each child needs to be considered in order to maximize the learning potential.

1. Read a riddle with a child and ask them to guess what it might be based on the descriptive clues.

2. Read a riddle with a child and ask them to guess what else rhymes with the clue.

3. Give each child a picture and word of a riddle. Read the riddle and have the children listen to see if their picture and word matches the riddle.

4. Choose a riddle that aligns with a book or topic of study and write it on a chart paper or project it digitally. At circle time or in small groups, work together to solve it.

5. Similar to the suggestions listed above but with a little twist. Give each child an answer card with a picture/word on it. Use these to let the children find who has the answer. Use the words at the back of this book to support this idea.

6. Digitally have the riddles on a projector with digital pictures/answers. Have the children find the correct match.

7. In small group or a learning center (with adult reading support as needed), have the riddles and answer cards separated on card stock. Let the children match them.

8. Make a copy of a riddle page and write the answers on a word bank sheet. Have the children use the word bank to write the answers on their sheet (Suggestion: Best used with children that are already reading.)

9. Review the Word Card activity section for more ideas.

10. Use the white space on each theme page to place post it notes as you monitor responses throughout the activity

11. For more ideas follow @AnitaVermeer27

Additional Ideas for Parents (or Educators):

Play a rhyming game when on the move such as in the car, or on a walk.

The game is simple by saying the word of an object you see or think of, and then taking turns saying as many words that rhymes as you can. It's okay if the words are not real words as the point is to practice the rhyming. For example, say you've seen a bus, then rhyming words could be gus, mus, hus, or wus.

If your child says a word that doesn't rhyme repeat the words and add a rhyme word. Then tell them the two that rhyme and the one that doesn't and then play again.

Or rather than focusing on rhyming, play what am I with your child by building on vocabulary using new adjectives and conceptual thinking. You can play this when you are on the go or when you are stuck waiting somewhere such as in a grocery store line or at a doctor's office.

How the game works is you tell your child "I'm thinking of a word that is (insert theme *such as a type of dessert)*". Then tell the child that you are going to give hints and they will have to guess. Then give the child a few clues along the way to help them guess. For example, "this type of dessert is round. This type of dessert is baked in the oven. This type of dessert is sliced into pieces to eat. What am I?"

Riddle Themes:

The following pages show popular Christian themes used with young children throughout bible studies. Each theme has 8 riddles.

For more themes check out one of these other books:

"Fun Seasonal Themes"
"Fun Popular Themes"
"Fun Popular Themes TOO!"
"What Am I? Riddles That Rhyme"

Adam and Eve's Garden

A place where many things can grow,
Like fruit or veggies that you know.
Rabbits need to beg your pardon,
When they eat from a _____.

An apple is one of these,
Very sweet attracting bees.
From a seed into a root,
On a tree it's called a _____.

The holy day you need to know,
How God had made it all to grow.
On this day you do your best,
To worship God and take a _____.

From the tree that Eve did take,
The apple from the talking snake.
This is not the way to win,
Disobeying is a _____.

This is a woman that God made,
For his love it could not fade.
God did not stop and would not leave,
'Till Adam had a friend named _____.

In a tree this creature hides,
As it slithers and it slides.
It told Eve something fake,
Because it was an evil _____.

This first thing God made for me,
He made the sun for all to see.
Up above to fullest height,
God created our day _____.

The second thing God did for us,
Was more than sun it was a plus.
This is where the birds can fly,
Up above in the _____.

Christmas

This lady had to travel far,
She was a mom without a car.
God's son is who she got to carry,
To Bethlehem her name was _____.

This farm building has some hay,
Lots of animals come this way.
Wool from sheep that could make yarn,
Is just one thing that's from a _____.

If you look up into the sky,
You'll see this twinkle really high.
The northern one may be real far,
But it shines bright cause it's a _____.

Jesus had this for a name,
Son of God was quite the fame.
Lots of angels came to sing,
Glory to the newborn _____.

An animal that you may know,
Has wool on it and it will grow.
Shave it off for you to keep,
It says baa 'cause it's a _____.

When he was born, he could not talk,
And he had to learn to walk.
But son of God there was no maybe,
Jesus was a newborn _____.

This is the place that Jesus lay,
When he was born on top of hay.
In bed he slept and had no danger,
With the animals in a _____.

A dad may call his kid a boy,
Showing love not with a toy.
God loved all not just this one,
That's why Jesus is his _____.

Daniel and the Lion

This is a feeling that you get,
Face your fear and you'll be set.
Daniel felt this in the cave,
He prayed to God, and he felt _____.

A king can make up any rule,
When he thinks it feels real cool.
Face the lions' scary claw
If you prayed, it was his _____.

In their mouth and on their head,
They are sharp and used when fed.
To a lion you are beef,
When they want to use their _____.

A type of cave or curvy rock,
Makes their home place by a block.
Lots of lions, maybe ten,
Live inside this called a _____.

This was someone with a crown,
And always wore an angry frown.
Jealousy was his big thing,
Mad at everyone he was _____.

This is something that we do,
To give thanks or when we're blue.
Daniel did this every day,
To honor God, he stopped to _____.

Daniel saw this animal there,
With a mane and roar to scare.
Say a prayer and don't start cryin',
If you're faced to see a _____.

This is a feeling that you get,
When you're alone, or scared I bet.
Daniel didn't shed a tear,
Because he didn't need to _____.

David and Goliath

David played this music thing,
Because the people liked to sing.
Sometimes dull or sometimes sharp,
These are sounds played on a _____.

David carried this around,
As the sheep ate off the ground.
It was a stick but do not laugh,
With the sheep he used a _____.

One of these got thrown around,
Made the giant get knocked down.
These are hard just like your bones,
David had five of these _____.

David went down to this place.
He heard God and said his grace.
He was alone without a team,
He got his pebbles from a _____.

This is a weapon David had,
To save himself and he was glad.
They thought it would not hurt a lot,
But David won with a _____.

This is full of love to give,
God, he gave his life to live.
Inside of him he has this part,
Really big it's David's _____.

Goliath has a spot that's weak,
And it is not on his cheek.
You're too little they all said,
But David hit him on his _____.

Really tall Goliath stood,
A big bully 'cause he could.
No other man could match his weight,
In total feet his height was _____.

Easter

On this thing is where he died,
Jesus arms were spread real wide.
God took his son not for a loss,
But for our sins upon the _____.

For our sins and love is why,
On a cross this man did die.
But all for love is how he sees us,
Back alive his name is _____.

We do some wrong things all the time,
But may forget that they're a crime.
Like the earth the anger spins,
So he died for our _____.

This was something on his head,
Made with thorns to hurt it's said.
Do not make your sad face frown,
When you're thinking of this _____.

This is a place we all can go,
Why Jesus died for us you know.
If you're sad then count to seven,
Stop and pray and think of _____.

Son of God we all did know,
So a miracle had to show.
With his love we all will thrive,
Because Jesus is now _____.

On a rose stem these are found,
And on his crown that made it round.
Lots of angry types of scorns,
Hurt our Jesus wearing _____.

Fold your hands to show you care,
Say your thanks and give your share.
Ask for forgiveness is the way,
If you sin, then you must _____.

Jonah and the Whale

On top of water this will go,
Use a sail or maybe row.
With a net the fish would flip,
When sailors worked inside a _____.

God saved Jonah this is true,
From the water that was blue.
Saved his life so no one frowned,
Cause Jonah nearly died and _____.

Jonah did this in the whale,
On his knees he could not fail.
'Thank you, God!' is what you say,
When you praise and when you _____.

A big splash this thing can make,
It swims afar not just the lake.
A big belly and a tail,
Jonah went inside a _____.

Trapped inside for many nights,
Made Jonah pray away his frights.
Inside the whale he could not see,
The days had totaled up to _____.

Lakes or rivers or the sea,
You can drink or swim in me.
You drink more when it is hotter,
Jonah fell into the _____.

In the sea this blows around,
And makes the water splash abound.
Sometimes the boat will need a save,
If it's hit with a big _____.

You cannot run from God you know,
He stays with you and where you go.
Pray to him when you are wrong,
And he will help to keep you _____.

Moses

In a basket this was found,
Tiny whimper was the sound.
God had said there was no maybe,
To save the life of this _____.

Some will say it's like the sea,
But named the Nile is the key.
It is the longest water giver,
In all of Egypt it's a _____.

These are lots of little things,
That swarmed around with their wings.
Needing Pharoah to stop his lies,
Came the plague with swarms of _____.

Ten Commandments were on these,
To share the word across the seas.
At the time there were no phones,
So Moses used these two big ___.

God used this to show a sign,
That his word was right in line.
A plant that burned but did not push,
The signal cast this burning _____.

A burning bush is no mistake,
God had said there's lots at stake.
He used this sign to show he's higher,
God had burned the bush with _____.

This was something in the way,
When people walked to get away.
Parting water was the key,
When people crossed the red _____.

This curved stick is what you use,
When God tells you to spread the news.
No one ever thought to laugh,
When they trusted Moses' _____.

Noah's Arc

Many colors you will see,
After rain then comes me.
Near the sun and clouds, you know,
God will send you a _____.

Another name for a boat,
This is something that can float.
In a flood or in the dark,
Noah made this giant _____.

Noah built this big and wide,
To fit the animals all inside.
An arc is something that can float,
God told Noah to build a _____.

When water covers up the land,
And God almighty gives his hand.
A lot of rain will make some mud,
But too much will make a _____.

This is a number more than one,
Because a pair can be fun.
Many animals Noah knew,
Had to come in pairs of _____.

A bird for Noah gave the word,
The rain had stopped from the lord.
A sign from God he sends his love,
This white bird is called a _____.

This is stuff we want to eat,
Like bread or fruit and some meat.
It didn't matter what the mood,
Noah knew to gather _____.

This is the water from the sky,
From the clouds and you know why.
Pray to God, it keeps you sane,
When you feel there's too much _____.

Fall

Slow or fast they're fun to ride,
Because the weather's nice outside.
With just two wheels if you like,
Ride and pedal on your _____.

Walk, or run, or go do this,
A forest trail, or path is bliss.
Lots to see and lots to like,
Explore the nature, take a _____.

Squirrels like to gather these,
They fall down from many trees.
They are not sharp like some thorns,
They're round and smooth _____.

Wool, or cotton is how I'm made,
Choose any color I won't fade.
I keep you warm, so you feel better,
On your chest, I am a _____.

This is food your mom might bake,
Or from the store you buy and take.
Pumpkin, apple treats are why,
A circle dessert is yummy _____.

When it's cold your shorts won't do,
These are long down to your shoe.
Maybe get these from your aunts,
A pair of jeans or sweat _____.

In September you start a new,
A new grade and teacher too.
Teachers, friends and books are cool,
When you learn and go to _____.

Many sizes and shapes we are,
All outside and on the car.
Lots of colors on the trees,
But we fall off since we are _____.

Winter

These are two things for your feet,
When there's snow down on the street.
Wear these when you wear snowsuits,
So feet stay dry in your _____.

Tiny flakes fall from above,
When this happens, you're in love.
Because you get to sled and go,
Outside to play in the _____.

Wear this on your head all day,
When you go outside to play.
It keeps you warm just like a cat,
And your ears 'cause it's a _____.

This is a type of winter storm,
Piles of snow will likely form.
Run and hide just like a lizard,
To stay safe if there's a _____.

Wear this outside so you can play,
Or in the car to school each day.
Zip it high up to your throat,
To stay warm with your _____.

Tiny little drops of ice,
They are hard and like dried rice.
From the sky these fall and flail,
They bang round 'cause it is _____.

I'm like some mittens, but I'm not,
Ten little spots is what I've got.
All your fingers find the loves,
When you wear this pair of _____.

An activity done for fun,
Blade on your foot, but not to run.
On the ice you cannot wait,
To get out and go and _____.

Spring

This is something with two wheels,
And riding it just gives you feels.
Sometimes you might not want to hike,
But ride on this 'cause it is a _____.

Many drops fall from the sky,
And an umbrella will keep you dry.
Wear some boots to keep you sane,
So you can play out in the _____.

Plants to eat is what you grow,
Some vegetables and food you know.
Without water the ground will harden,
So take care of your own _____.

Many colors you can see,
On the ground or on a tree.
They say that after April showers,
Then comes May with lots of _____.

Bugs and flies are called these things,
Many shapes and many wings.
We wonder what might happen next.
Crawl or fly they are _____.

This a beetle that is round,
Near some aphids it is found.
They are cute not like a slug,
Red wings we call a _____.

Sometimes one or sometimes two,
Weeks of these are just for you.
A lot of time in school you make,
So days off is called Spring _____.

In the spring you like to play,
Outside a lot and every day.
When it's not raining, it is fun,
And may be hot out in the _____.

Summer

In the summer you go to play,
On the slide or swing to sway.
Ready, set, go on your mark,
Lots to play with at the _____.

These are people that you like,
To go play with or ride a bike.
The fun you have will never end,
Because each one is your _____.

In the sun your hair gets hot,
And sunscreen might not get this spot.
On your head for when you chat,
You wear this 'cause it's a _____.

With your family you will go,
To a place you may not know.
In a car, a plane or ship,
You may take a family _____.

Insects are just what these all are,
They are outside and by the car.
If you're scared then get some hugs,
From your mom, not these they're _____.

This is found by ocean water,
On your feet it will feel hotter.
Sand is everywhere in your reach,
When you're sitting at the _____.

Play some games and pack some food,
At the park or neighborhood.
Have some fun and play for kicks,
With family or friends at _____.

In the summer the sun is hot,
So finding me is what your taught.
Under a tree is how I'm made,
When I block the sun, you'll find some _____.

Weather

This makes everything get wet,
You'll use umbrellas I can bet.
On your house or in the plains,
Stuff gets wet when it _____.

Many colors you can see,
When the rain has left to be.
Maybe some gold will be for show,
At the end of a _____.

Very bright and big you know,
It is hot so out you go.
Everyone must have some fun,
When you play out in the _____.

Little flakes of white will fall,
When it does, you'll have a ball.
Melts in heat you must know,
Keep it cold 'cause it is _____.

These are clouds that sit real low,
And make it damp and dark you know.
Not the weather for you to jog,
'Cause it's hard to see in _____.

These are things that fall on down,
Hard little pellets make you frown.
You'll hear it clang against the rail,
As it is ice that we call _____.

This light you see up in the sky,
From stormy weather is reason why.
The sound from this is quite frightenin'
After thunder comes the _____.

Up in the sky fluffy and white,
Or the storm ones are a sight.
Pretend a shape is what's allowed,
When you look up at a _____.

Which Rhymes Matching Activities

These activities can be done independently or together with an adult. For independent work you can model how to complete the worksheet and then copy the pages for the children to do on their own. Or, if you'd like to provide more adult support or prompts, you can copy the activity on a white board or chart paper and complete it together.

Summer Sample:

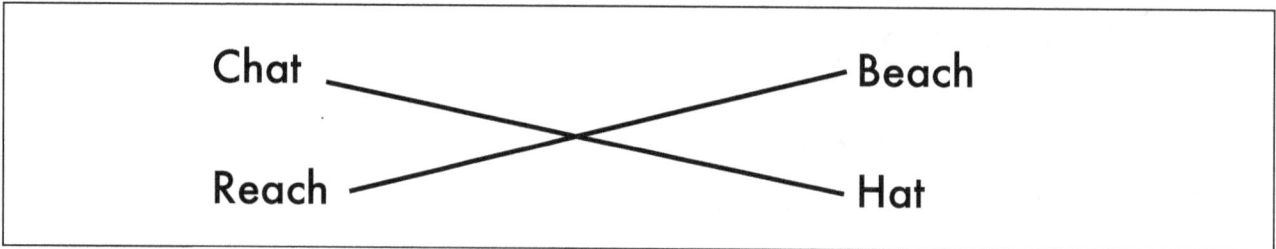

On your head for when you chat,
You wear this 'cause it's a <u>hat</u>.

Sand is everywhere in your reach,
When you're sitting at the <u>beach</u>.

ADAM AND EVE'S GARDEN

Draw a line to match an Adam and Eve's Garden word with a rhyming word.

Height	Eve
Leave	Snake
Fake	Sky
Fly	Light
Root	Fruit

Complete the Adam and Eve's Garden rhymes.

It told Eve something fake,
Because it was an evil _____.

This is where the birds can fly,
Up above in the _____.

God did not stop and would not leave,
'Till Adam had a friend named _____.

CHRISTMAS

Draw a line to match a Christmas word with a rhyming word.

Far	Manger
Carry	Star
Sing	Mary
Danger	Sheep
Keep	King

Complete the Christmas rhymes.

In bed he slept and had no danger,
With the animals in a _____.

The northern one may be real far,
But it shines bright cause it's a _____.

Lots of angels came to sing,
Glory to the newborn _____.

Riddles & Rhymes: Christian Themes

DANIEL AND THE LION

Draw a line to match a Daniel and the Lion word with a rhyming word.

Beef	Pray
Tear	Fear
Cave	Law
Day	Teeth
Claw	Brave

Complete the Daniel and the Lion rhymes.

> Daniel did this every day,
> To honor God, he stopped to _____.

> Daniel felt this in the cave,
> He prayed to God, and he felt _____.

> To a lion you are beef,
> When they want to use their _____.

DAVID AND GOLIATH

Draw a line to match a David and Goliath word with a rhyming word.

Sharp	Laugh
Team	Harp
Staff	Stones
Weight	Eight
Bones	Stream

Complete the David and Goliath rhymes.

He was alone without a team,
He got his pebbles from a _____.

It was a stick but do not laugh,
With the sheep he used a _____.

Sometimes dull or sometimes sharp,
These are sounds played on a _____.

EASTER

Draw a line to match an Easter word with a rhyming word.

Scorns	Heaven
Frown	Cross
Seven	Pray
Way	Thorns
Loss	Crown

Complete the Easter rhymes.

If you're sad then count to seven,
Stop and pray and think of _____.

God took his son not for a loss,
But for our sins upon the _____.

With his love we all will thrive,
Because Jesus is now _____.

JONAH AND THE WHALE

Draw a line to match a Jonah and the Whale word with a rhyming word.

Flip	Whale
Hotter	Pray
See	Ship
Say	Three
Tail	Water

Complete the Jonah and the Whale rhymes.

A big belly and a tail,
Jonah went inside a _____.

'Thank you, God!' is what you say,
When you praise and when you _____.

With a net the fish would flip,
When sailors worked inside a _____.

MOSES

Draw a line to match a Moses word with a rhyming word.

Phones	Sea
Higher	Baby
Maybe	Stones
Key	Bush
Push	Fire

Complete the Moses rhymes.

God had said there was no maybe,
To save the life of this _____.

He used this sign to show he's higher,
God had burned the bush with _____.

At the time there were no phones,
So Moses used these two big _____.

NOAH'S ARC

Draw a line to match a Noah's Arc word with a rhyming word.

Float	Two
Dark	Arc
Mud	Dove
Knew	Boat
Love	Flood

Complete the Noah's Arc rhymes.

An arc is something that can float,
God told Noah to build a _____.

Many animals Noah knew,
Had to come in pairs of _____.

A sign from God he sends his love,
This white bird is called a _____.

FALL

Draw a line to match a Fall word with a rhyming word.

Like	Hike
Trees	Bike
Why	Pie
Cool	School
Like	Leaves

Complete the Fall rhymes.

Pumpkin, apple treats are why,
A circle dessert is yummy _____.

Teachers, friends and books are cool,
When you learn and go to _____.

With just two wheels if you like,
Ride and pedal on your _____.

WINTER

Draw a line to match a Winter word with a rhyming word.

Go	Hat
Wait	Blizzard
Throat	Coat
Cat	Snow
Lizard	Skate

Complete the Winter rhymes.

Zip it high up to your throat,
To stay warm with your _____.

Because you get to sled and go,
Outside to play in the _____.

On the ice you cannot wait,
To get out and go and _____.

SPRING

Draw a line to match a Spring word with a rhyming word.

Slug	Garden
Hike	Rain
Sane	Flowers
Harden	Bike
Showers	Bug

Complete the Spring rhymes.

> Wear some boots to keep you sane,
> So you can play out in the _____.
>
> Without water the ground will harden,
> So take care of your own _____.
>
> They say that after April showers,
> Then comes May with lots of _____.

SUMMER

Draw a line to match a Summer word with a rhyming word.

Chat	Park
Mark	Trip
Reach	Friend
End	Hat
Ship	Beach

Complete the summer rhymes.

> The fun you have will never end,
> Because each one is your _____.

> On your head for when you chat,
> You wear this 'cause it's a _____.

> Sand is everywhere in your reach,
> When you're sitting at the _____.

WEATHER

Draw a line to match a Weather word with a rhyming word.

Jog	Sun
Fun	Fog
Know	Snow
Plains	Cloud
Allowed	Rains

Complete the weather rhymes.

Everyone must have some fun,
When you play out in the _____.

Melts in heat you must know,
Keep it cold 'cause it is _____.

Not the weather for you to jog,
'Cause it's hard to see in _____.

Word Card Matching Game

These word cards are developed for you as a tool. They can support you with the rhyme riddles or you can use them in new ways to build vocabulary or literacy skills. Typically, a child would need to have the decoding skills or sight word memory in order to be successful at using these word cards as they are printed. However, there are ways to simplify the use of these cards, so they work well with younger children or beginner readers.

Activity Idea for Parents or Educators:

Using these cards without pictures can save you time in preparation work such as cutting or sorting pictures and will also help the child build some connection that each word has a meaning.

- Copy these onto card stock and cut the word cards, separating the themes. If you are working with larger groups of children you might want to either make two copies of each theme, or plan to do two themes at time.

- Give each child a card and read them the word or if working with just one child you can give all 8 cards to one child.

- Have each child draw a picture of the word they received on the card on the front next to the printed word. For example, Child A may have a bike to draw, Child B some acorns, Child C some pie and so on. If you are working with just one child, then you can have the child draw on all 8 cards.

- Unless time permits to do the next step on the same day, collect the cards or have the children put them in a safe space to do the next part on another day. (Note: Read the next step to decide if you want the child to put their name on the back or not before you collect them.)

- On another day, have the cards ready for a rhyme reading session. You may choose to put them in the center of a table and use them with an individual child or small group of children, or on a pocket chart with a larger group, or perhaps hand them back out to the class.

- As you read a rhyme have the children listen for the clue to word and encourage them to use the pictures to help them solve the riddle. If you handed the cards out to the individual child, you could have them raise their card in the air when they hear their rhyme.

Challenging Activity Ideas:

- If you'd like to make this activity more challenging, you can mix two or more sets of theme cards together and have the child identify the right card for the right rhyme.

- Or to support classification skills, you could encourage the child to sort the words into piles based on the topic such as sorting words that are Halloween, or words that are Christmas.

- For older children that are ready, you could encourage them to put the cards in alphabetical order or use them as flash cards to read or spell.

- Have the children draw the pictures on separate index cards and then play matching games to pair up the word with the picture.

Adam and Eve's Garden

garden	fruit
rest	sin
snake	eve
light	sky

Page intentionally left blank.

Christmas

son	manger
sheep	baby
king	star
barn	Mary

Page intentionally left blank.

Daniel and the Lion

teeth	pray
king	den
brave	law
fear	lion

Page intentionally left blank.

David and Goliath

stream	stones
heart	slingshot
harp	staff
eight	head

Page intentionally left blank.

Easter

Jesus	cross
crown	sins
pray	thorns
alive	heaven

Page intentionally left blank.

Jonah and the Whale

pray	drowned
whale	ship
strong	wave
three	water

Page intentionally left blank.

Noah's Arc

rainbow	arc
flood	boat
two	dove
rain	food

Page intentionally left blank.

Moses

river	fire
baby	flies
staff	bush
sea	stones

Page intentionally left blank.

Fall

bike	hike
sweater	acorns
school	leaves
pants	pie

Page intentionally left blank.

Winter

snow	hat
boots	blizzard
skate	hail
coat	gloves

Page intentionally left blank.

Spring

bike	rain
garden	flowers
break	insects
sun	bugs

Page intentionally left blank.

Summer

park	friend
hat	trip
bugs	beach
picnics	shade

Page intentionally left blank.

Weather

rain	rainbow
snow	sun
fog	hail
cloud	lightning

Page intentionally left blank.

Answers

Adam and Eve's Garden
Garden
Fruit
Rest
Sin
Eve
Snake
Light
Sky

Christmas
Mary
Barn
Star
King
Sheep
Baby
Manger
Son

Daniel and the Lion
Brave
Law
Teeth
Den
King
Pray
Lion
Fear

David and Goliath
Harp
Staff
Stones
Stream
Slingshot
Heart
Head
Eight

Easter
Cross
Jesus
Sins
Crown
Heaven
Alive
Thorns
Pray

Jonah and the Whale
Ship
Drowned
Pray
Whale
Three
Water
Wave
Strong

Moses
Baby
River
Flies
Bush
Fire
Sea
Staff
Stones

Noah's Arc
Rainbow
Arc
Boat
Flood
Two
Dove
Food
Rain

Fall
Bike
Hike
Acorns
Sweater
Pie
Pants
School
Leaves

Winter
Boots
Snow
Hat
Blizzard
Coat
Hail
Gloves
Skate

Weather
Rain
Rainbow
Sun
Snow
Fog
Hail
Lightning
Cloud

Spring
Bike
Rain
Garden
Flowers
Insects
Bugs
Break
Sun

Summer
Park
Friend
Hat
Trip
Bugs
Beach
Picnics
Shade

About the Author

Anita Vermeer, M.Ed. is an author, parent, coach, and certified teacher with over 25 years of experience working for young children.

Anita believes that the potential in each child is enhanced through engagement and connection. Her author journey began when she wrote rhyming riddles and used them with preschoolers. It was then in Ontario, Canada that the idea was born.

Years later, after building curriculum in early childhood school systems, and becoming a parent, Anita felt inspired to publish and promote early literacy in a new way.

With her background in early childhood, and belief that children are naturally curious, you can be sure that Anita's resources are educational and engaging.

To learn more visit **www.AnitaVermeer27.com**
and follow **@AnitaVermeer27**

Other Books Written by Anita Vermeer:

- *Fun Seasonal Theme*
- *Fun Popular Themes*
- *Fun Popular Themes TOO!*
- What Am I? Riddles That Rhyme
- Play and Learning Activities That Engage Toddlers and Preschoolers

www.ingramcontent.com/pod-product-compliance
Lightning Source LLC
Chambersburg PA
CBHW081626100526
44590CB00021B/3614